Happy Holiday Riddles to YOU!

By Joanne E. Bernstein and Paul Cohen
Illustrated by Meyer Seltzer

Albert Whitman & Company
Niles, Illinois

Also by Joanne E. Bernstein and Paul Cohen

Un-Frog-Gettable Riddles
Unidentified Flying Riddles

Library of Congress Cataloging in Publication Data

Bernstein, Joanne E.
  Happy holiday riddles to you!

  Summary: Includes one hundred riddles about a wide
variety of major and minor holidays both religious and secular.
    1. Riddles, Juvenile. 2. Holidays—Juvenile humor.
[1. Riddles. 2. Holidays—Wit and humor] I. Cohen, Paul,
1945- II. Seltzer, Meyer, ill. III. Title.
PN6371.5.B395 1985 818'.5402   85-717
ISBN 0-8075-3154-5 (lib. bdg.)

Text © 1985 by Joanne E. Bernstein and Paul Cohen.
Illustrations © 1985 by Meyer Seltzer.
Published in 1985 by Albert Whitman & Company, Niles, Illinois.
Published simultaneously in Canada by
General Publishing, Limited, Toronto.
All rights reserved. Printed in U.S.A.

Which is the slowest moving Chinese year?
The year of the drag-on.

What do telephones do on January 1?
They ring in the New Year.

Why don't we feel the cold on New Year's Eve?
Because we spend the night toasting each other.

What does a caterpillar do on New Year's Day?
It turns over a new leaf.

When can a monkey turn into a rooster?
On Chinese New Year.

Groundhog Day

When does the frog come out of his hole?
Groundfrog Day.

What happens when he sees his shadow?
You get six more weeks of warts.

What happens when you see the shadow of your television antenna?
You get six more weeks of reruns.

The more you take away, the larger it grows. What is it?
A hole in the ground.

What holiday does a truck driver celebrate?
Road Hog Day.

What's the best day for squeezing the soil?
Groundhug Day.

Lincoln's Birthday

If Lincoln were alive today, what would he be most famous for?
He'd be the world's oldest living man.

How many legs has a mule if you call a tail a leg?
Four. Even if you call a tail a leg, it is still a tail. (This riddle was made up by Lincoln.)

Teacher: Henry, can you give me Lincoln's Gettysburg Address?
Henry: No, but his Washington address was 1600 Pennsylvania Avenue.

Teacher: What great event happened in 1809?
Jane: Abraham Lincoln was born.
Teacher: Correct. And what great event happened in 1812?
Jane: Lincoln had his third birthday.

Father: Just think, Son, when Abe Lincoln was your age, he was splitting rails for a living.
Son: Yes, I know, Dad, and when he was YOUR age, he was president of the United States.

Sally: Did you know you can't send mail to Roosevelt?
Tom: No, why not?
Sally: Because he's dead. But you can send mail to Lincoln.
Tom: But he's dead, too.
Sally: I know, but he left his Gettysburg Address.

Valentine's Day

What do sailors give each other on Valentine's Day?
Forget-me-knots.

What did the stamp say to the envelope?
"I've grown attached to you."

What should you get from a funny valentine?
A heart-y-har-har.

Where do you put valentines to boys?
In the male box.

Ted: What's the difference between a mailbox and a kangaroo?
Bob: Well, if you don't know, remind me not to give you any valentines to mail.

What travels around the world but stays in a corner?
A stamp.

What does an envelope say when you lick it?
Nothing. It just shuts up.

What happens to letter carriers who get old?
They lose their zip.

Washington's Birthday

Which American had the biggest family?
Washington, because he was the father of his country.

If Washington were alive today, why couldn't he throw a silver dollar across the Potomac?
Because a dollar doesn't go as far as it used to.

Why did George Washington chop down the cherry tree?
Stumps me.

Three men jumped off the Washington Bridge, and one didn't get his hair wet. How come?
He was bald.

What did George Washington's father say when he saw George's report card?
"George, you're going down in history."

What did Washington say to his men before crossing the Delaware by boat?
"Get in."

What does _Washington, D.C.,_ stand for?
Washington, Daddy of His Country.

If you washed a pound of clothes each day for 2,000 days, what would you be doing?
Washington.

What's Irish and sits on the lawn in October?
Jack O'Lantern.

What's Irish and stays out on the lawn all summer?
Paddy O'Furniture.

Why do frogs wish St. Patrick's Day came more often?
They're always wearing green.

What saint's day do hockey players enjoy?
St. Hat Trick's Day.

April Fool's Day

What holiday do babies love?
April Drool's Day.

What holiday does Oliver Twist love?
April Gruel's Day.

Why are the scouts so tired on April Fool's Day?
Because they've just had a thirty-one day March.

What would happen if you moved Halloween from the fall to the spring?
You'd get April Ghoul's Day.

Passover

Son: Dad, have you ever been to Egypt?
Dad: No, why?
Son: Well then, where did you get Mummy?

Why can you only have ten matzos on Passover?
Because you can't have 'leaven.

What would happen if you threw a white rock into the Red Sea?
It would get wet.

What are the little rivers called that run into the Nile?
The juve-niles.

How did Moses describe Egypt's treatment of his people?
Un-pharaoh.

What grade did God give the Pharaoh?
A big red "C."

Who carries colored eggs in his trunk?
The Easter elephant.

What holiday near Easter is like a hand?
Palm Sunday.

What state is a church service?
Mass. (Massachusetts)

How can you tell where the Easter Bunny's been?
Eggs mark the spot.

On what holiday does the President have Chinese food?
Easter. He always has an egg roll on the lawn.

What's the best way to send a letter to the Easter Bunny?
Hare mail.

Mother and Father's Day

What do monsters do on the second Sunday in May?
Give presents to their mummies.

What was it that Adam and Eve never saw, never had, and still gave two of to their children?
Parents.

Why is there a Mother's Day, a Father's Day, but not a Son's Day?
Because there is a Sunday every week.

When does a caterpillar give its mommy a present?
Moth-er's Day.

Flag Day

What do patriotic monkeys wave on Flag Day?
Star-spangled bananas.

When Betsy Ross was asked to make a flag, how did she feel about it?
Sew-sew.

What gets up in the morning and waves all day?
The flag.

Why did Betsy Ross go to the eye doctor?
She had started seeing stars and stripes.

What was Betsy Ross's reply when she was asked if the flag was ready?
"Give me a minute, man."

What made Francis Scott Key famous?
He knew all the verses to the "Star Spangled Banner."

Do you know why there are stars on the U.S. flag and a sun on the Japanese flag?
Because it's daytime in Japan when it's nighttime in the U.S.

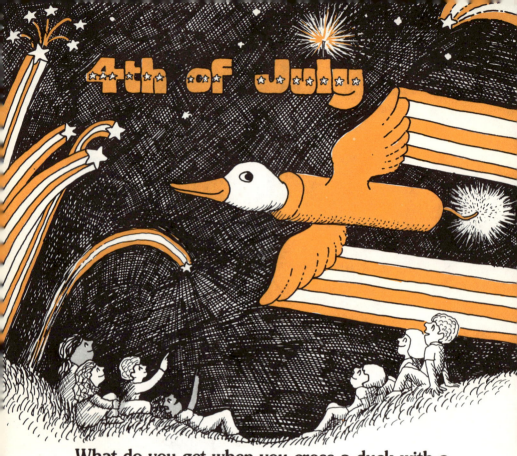

What do you get when you cross a duck with a flame on the Fourth of July?
A fire quacker.

Why does Uncle Sam wear red, white, and blue suspenders?
To hold up his pants.

What is the Declaration of Independence?
A note excusing you from school.

What meal did the Revolutionists serve to catch spies?
Chicken Catch-a-Tory.

What would you say if everyone in the U.S. sneezed at the same time?
"God bless America!"

What was purple and ruled the colonies?
Grape Britain.

What are the last two words of the national anthem?
"Play ball."

What's worse than singing the "Star Spangled Banner" for hours?
Singing the "Stars and Stripes" forever.

Columbus Day

Was it expensive for Columbus to travel to America?
No, he traveled over three thousand miles on a single galleon.

What was the first bus to cross the Atlantic?
Colum-bus.

When Columbus discovered America, where did he first stand?
On his feet.

Sue: I can trace my ancestors all the way back to Columbus.
Sarah: Wow! To 1492?
Sue: No, to Columbus, Ohio.

What do birds say on Halloween?
"Twick or tweet."

On what holiday do you scream?
Holler-een.

Why do you drill holes in hot dogs in October?
To make hollow wienies.

What kind of mistake does a trick-or-treater make?
A boo-boo.

How does a witch tell time?
With a witch watch.

Is Halloween celebrated throughout the U.S.?
Yes, from ghost to ghost.

Why is Halloween such a happy holiday?
It's when the spirits rise.

Thanksgiving

What do you get if you cross a turkey with an ostrich?
A Thanksgiving bird that buries its head in the mashed potatoes.

What do you get when you cross a turkey with a hippopotamus?
A Thanksgiving dinner requiring six hundred pounds of stuffing.

Who's never hungry at Thanksgiving dinner?
The turkey. He's always stuffed.

How is a turkey like a ghost?
It's always a gobblin'.

If April showers bring May flowers, what do May flowers bring?
Pilgrims.

What kind of music did the Pilgrims like?
Plymouth Rock.

What is Dracula's favorite holiday?
Fangsgiving.

Why were the Indians the first people in North America?
They had reservations.

Where did the first corn come from?
The stalk brought it.

If the Pilgrims came over on the Mayflower, how did the barbers arrive?
On clipper ships.

Chanukah

Why did the boy's mother knit him three socks for Chanukah?
He'd grown another foot.

What do Jewish people always do before they light the Chanukah candles?
Strike a match.

Why did Johnny eat honey on Chanukah?
To honor the Macca-bees.

Christmas

What do Eskimos buy at Christmas?
Christmas seals.

A Russian named Rudolph looked out the window one morning and announced, "It's raining."
His wife looked out also and said, "No, it's sleeting."
"It's raining," insisted the husband. "Rudolph the Red knows rain, dear."

Who gives everyone five cents on Christmas?
St. Nickel-as.

Knock, knock.
Who's there?
Amory.
Amory who?
Amory Christmas and a Happy New Year.

Knock, knock.
Who's there?
Hannah.
Hannah who?
Hannah partridge in a pear tree.

Who dresses in red, carries a bag of toys, and falls down the chimney?
Santa Klutz.

Why did Santa use only seven reindeer this year?
He left Comet at home to clean the sink.

Why does the Christmas alphabet have only twenty-five letters?
No-el.

Of what use is a reindeer?
To make the flowers grow, sweetie.

When do you use mistletoe?
On Kissmas.

Knock, knock.
Who's there?
Doughnut.
Doughnut who?
Doughnut open until Christmas.

What does Tarzan sing at Christmas?
"Jungle Bells."

What is claustrophobia?
Fear of Santa.

Why are gloves the best Christmas present in England?
The next day is Boxing Day.

What happened to your Christmas tree?
It's pining away.

What would you get if Minnehaha married Santa?
Minnehahahoho.

What nationality is Santa Claus?
North Polish.

How is a lion in the desert like Christmas?
It has Sandy Claws.

Why couldn't Jane go to Amy's birthday party?
The invitation said four to seven, and she was ten.

What did the burglar give his wife for her birthday?
A stole.

Why is it so much fun to sleep on a ship?
It's always your berth-day.

How can you live eighty years but have only twenty birthdays?
Be born on February 29th.

Teacher: When's your birthday?
Student: November 13.
Teacher: What year?
Student: Every year.

Why does Father Time wear bandages?
Because day breaks and night falls.

Name four cities that are holidays.
Lincoln, Nebraska; Washington, D.C.;
Independence, Missouri; Columbus, Ohio.

Why was everyone so jumpy in 1984?
It was a leap year.

Why is the calendar sad?
Because its days are numbered.

What's the only kind of food you can eat on Yom Kippur?
Fast food.

What day of the year is a command to go forward?
March 4th.

On what holiday do you hurry home?
Rush Hashanah.

**We honor two presidents in the winter.
When do we honor a king?**
On January 15th. (The birthday of Martin Luther King, Jr.)

On what holiday are the most babies born?
Labor Day.

What's the very first thing people give up for Lent?
Mardi Gras.

What number has its own day?
2sday.

What do you get when it rains on Veteran's Day?
A soaking vet.

Do cats have their special holiday?
Sure, Purr-im.

Why is Election Day the best day to explore the Arctic?
It's when the polls (poles) are open.

Why is this the last riddle in the book?
Because we're off on holidays!

We vacation mainly in Maine
Love,
Joanne

We spend our vacations mainly across the main, in Europe.
Love,
Paul and Marie

I love to draw — but there are things I'd rudder do. We'll meet soon in another book, O.K.?
Love
Meyer

P.S. Those are my daughters
Elisa and Margo